Other books

-Our Story of a Twin Flame Union

- Akashic Realm Journeys

-A Walk with the Neteru: a Kemetic Yearly Calendar

Dua (Thanks and Praises)

Dua Pa Neter, Nebetcher, the Creative force that exist within all things. You are the spark within me that connects us all.

Dua, to my Ancestors, who suffered and achieved so much. Without you I wouldn't be here to do what I do now.

Dua, to the Elders, Thank you for sharing your Wisdom and walking your journeys.

Finally, Much Thanks to my family who inspire me in all that I do. To my King Uraeus Ophaughnie Neteru Amaru Anuwi Heru-Ur, Thank you for your support always. To my daughters (and any other future children that Will come thru), Maati Takala Merit-Heru and Naeemah Amari Nefertah, may you always know magic in your lives.

Table of Contents

-Whats in a name?

-How to pick a Kemetic name for yourself

-Common factors

-A list of names

      -Divine Feminine names

      -Divine Masculine names

-Suggested reading

-Bibliography

Whats in a Name?

Ra embued the first creatures and objects with energy by speaking their names. He spoke himself into existence with an uttering of RA! The name in some traditions around the world is so sacred that each child is born with two or more. One of them is their common name. Another is for Spiritual use only. The Kemetic (and other African peoples) knew the importance of naming ones child something that truly fit them. They would name the child for their Divine Purpose, Destiny, and or Talents and Gifts they've brought to share with the World. The Ancestors also knew that names carry a certain vibration or Energetic Signature. Names were not picked as they are in today's modern society. There were No Jr's for the sake of naming your child after yourself. Last names were not passed down (which is a way to show ownership of a child but not a way to identify who the child is, and what works their here to complete)... Names were not picked due to trends or what sounded good. For instance, the name Ankhen Aton; meaning Life of Aton. This is a name given to show a closeness to the Neter Aton. The kings, when coronated, were given five different names to be used on different occasions. A name could be used in spells and magic, to give good fortune or to curse. So when one picks, or is given, a Spiritual name it is important to truly look into the meaning of that Energy Signature, as that will be the Vibration you'll be carrying.

In many Hindu yogic paths ones Guru (a holy person or teacher) may give you your Spiritual name. In certain Neo Pagan practices you are granted your name by the High Priest or

Priestess of the coven you attend. Shamans all around the world are known to rename people after they have gone through certain rites of passage. This is to show a transition from the person you once were to who you are now, and who you'll become. You carried a different energy at the beginning of your journey then you do at the end of it. Examples of Hindu Spiritual names are Ram Das, Parvati, Kali, Krishna Das (some of these are famous people). Examples of Neo Pagan names are Ambrosia Kat Dragon (my name when I was Wiccan), Kali Sage Dragon (My Mother's name). My mother picked this name because Kali is a Goddess of transformation. Sage is both cleansing and a word meaning wise. Dragon is a mythical creature that shows fierce transformation while using fire to cleanse.

How to pick a Kemetic Name for yourself

"Nuk pa Neter aah Neter uah asha ren (I am that same god, the supreme one, who has myriad of mysterious names)"- Prt M Hru

A Kemetic name like any other Spiritual name should be a reflection of the person it belongs to. The name should reflect the Immortal Neter that is living a mortal life . I will use some friends and family members as examples of what a Spiritual name can look like.

Starting off with my king who's full Spiritual name is **Uraeus Ophaughnie Neteru Amaru Anuwi Heru-Ur**. Uraeus is a name of a Kemetic serpent goddess who is seen as the eye of Ra (found on the headresses of kings) she also represents the kundalini energy. Ophaughnie or the Ophaughn are Angelic Sky Beings that have returned or arrived. Neteru, which is where the word Nature comes from, are Divine Beings or Gods in the Ancient Kemetic tongue. Amaru meaning Unconditional Love (this is where the Latin word Amor, meaning Love, came from). The Anuwi, which are also Angelic Beings in Human Form. Heru-Ur is Heru the great, or Heru The Elder. He is the brother of Ausar and Auset, not their son.

Our oldest daughter's name is **Maati Takala Merit-Heru**. Her name starts off with the laws of Maat and keeping true to those. Takala (not Kemetic) means corn husk. Merit

Heru, means beloved of Heru. Our second daughter's birth name is her Spiritual name. Her name is **Naeemah Amari Nefertah** which means benevolent one of unconditional love, (Amari is a varient of Amaru) here to bring beauty to the Gaia (earth). Her name is her Mission as was written in the stars, Celestial bodies, and was Scribed by her father, Uraeus, while doing her natal charts.

My Spiritual name also comes from my Destiny as written in the Stars, and read from my natal charts. This name is **UaaHebebaiKa RekhNefu**. Uaa comes from my north node and shows my Journey for Peace and Meditation. HebaiKa shows my Playful Spirit. RekhNefu also shows my Journey for Wisdom and Freedom.

A family friend was renamed by his father during his 16th year of life. His new name was to be **Taaluta Re HeruKhuti**. Taaluta is a mixture of two Kemetic names Taa meaning earth/grounded and Luta meaning spiratic. Re is a varient of the Sun god Ra's name. Finally HeruKhuti is Heru in the horizon. Knowing this Brother, no name could describe him any better.

Below are some names that are traditionally Kemetic. There is no way to list all the Kemetic names ever used but this is a good supply to start with. A lot of the names have common factors or words to add to their meanings. Some of those factors are listed below also.

Common Factors:

Ankh- (AH nkh) Life

Seneb- (See neb) Health

Mose- (Mo say/ mos) Child

Sa- (Sah) Son

Saet- (sah et) Daughter

Hetep/ Hotep- (He-tep/Hoe-tep) Peace or pleased

Merit- (Mare-eet) Beloved (female)

Nefer/ Nefor- (Neh-fer/Neh-fer) Good, beauty, beautiful

Ib/Ab- (eeb/Ahb) Heart

Ka- (Kah) Soul

Mes- (Mess) Child (feminine)

Tawy- (Tah wee) two lands (referring to upper and lower Kemet)

Wer/ Ur- (Wer/ ur) Great one or elder

Rkht/ Rkhty- (Rech/ Rech tee) To know

Name of your personal Neter/ guide and or your relationship to them

Name of your place of birth

Name of the season or festival you were born or conceived during

A list of names

Divine Feminine names

A

Aat- (Ay aht) Great one

AatSenut- (Ay aht se noot) Eldest of sisters

AahHotep- (Ee ayh hoe-tep) The moon is pleased

AahMose-(Ee ayh mo say/ ee ayh mos) Child of the moon

Amen emOpet- (Ah men em oh pet/ I-men em oh pet/ Ah moon em oh pet) Amen at the Opet festival

Amenirdis-(Ah men ear dees/ I-men ear dees) She was given to Amun

Aneksi- (Ahn ek see) She belongs to me

AnkhesenAmen- (An kh es en Ah men/ An kh es en I-men) Her life is for Amun

AnkhesenAten- (An kh es en Ah ten) Her life is for Aten

AnkhesenmeriRe- (An kh es en mary Rah/ an kh es en mary ray) Her life is of the beloved of Ra

AnkhesenpaAten- (An kh es en pah ah ten) Her life is of Aten

AnkhesenRe- (An kh es en rah/ an kh es en ray) Her life is of Ra

Ankhmutes- (An kh moot es)Her mother lives

AnkhnesNeferHotep- (An kh nes neh-fer hoe-tep) Living through the beauty of peace

AnkhnesNeferibRa- (An kh nes neh-fer eeb rah/ an kh nes neh-fer ray) Living through the beautiful heart of Ra

Ashayt-(Ah shay et) She who poseses abundance

B

Baket- (Bahk et) Handmaden

BaketAmen- (Bahk et Ah men/ Bahk et Imen/ Bahk et Ah moon) Handmaiden of Amen

BaketAten- (Bahk et Ah ten) Handmaiden of Aten

BaketMut-(Bahk et Moot) Handmaiden of Mut

BaketRe- (Bahk et ray/ bahk et rah) Handmaiden of Ra

BaketWeret- (Bahk et wer et) Handmaiden of the Great one

Benerib-(Ben er eeb) Sweet of heart

BintAnath- (Bent ah-nath) Daughter of Anath

H

Hatshepsut- (Haht shep-soot) Formost of noble women

Hebai- (He bay ee) Playful/ playing

Hebaika- (He bay ee ka) Playful spirit / playing spirit

Hebeny-(Heh beny) Ebony

Hedjet- (Hed jet) Splindid

Heka-(heck ah) Magic or words of power

Hemetra-(Hem-et Ra/ Hem-et ray) Servant or priestess of Ra

Henut- (Heh noot) Mistress

Henutah- (Heh noot tah) Mistress of the palace

Henutmerut-(Heh noot mer-oot) Mistress of love

Henutnofert- (Heh noot no fert) Beautiful mistress

Henutskhemu- (Heh noot s-chem oo) Mistress of powers

Henutsen- (Hen noot sen) Our mistress

Henuttamenhu-(Heh noot tah men who) Mistress of lower Kemet

Henuttaneb- (Heh noot tah neb) Mistress of all lands

Henuttashemau- (Heh nut ash em-ay-oo) Mistress of upper Kemet

Henuttawy-(Heh noot tah we) Mistress of the two lands

Heruben-(Hair oo ben) Replendent sky

HesetRe-(He set rah/ he set ray) Favored by Ra

HetepenAmen-(Het ep en Ah men/ Het ep en I-men/ Het ep en Ah moon) Peace of Amun

Hetepet-(He tep et) Peaceful

I

IityMeritHotep-(Eetee mare eet ho tep) Welcome beloved of peace

Iset- (Ee set) A form of Auset

Isetemankh- (Ee set em an kh)The living Auset

Isetemheb-(Ee set em heb) Auset on jubilee

Isetnedjmet-(Ee set nej met) Auset is lovely

Isetnofret- (Ee set no fret) Auset is beautiful

Isetweret-(Ee set wer et) Auset is great

Iymeritnebes- (Ee mar eet neb es) Here comes the beloved of her lord

IymeritneHetep- (Ee mar eet ne he tep) Here comes the beloved of peace

Iyneferti- (Ee nef er tee) Here comes the beauty

K

KaMaat- (Kah May aht) Soul of truth

KasMut- (Kah moot) Her soul belongs to Mut

khenemetAmen-(Khen em et ah men/ khen em et ah moon/ khen em et I-men) United with Amen

khenemet-nefer-hedjet- (Khen em et ne fer hej et) United with the beautiful white one

Khenememet-nefer-es- (Khe hem em et ne fer es) United with her beauty

Khuit-(Khe oo it) Protected

M

MaatkaRe- (May aht kah rah, may aht kah ray) Truth is the soul of Ra

Maati- (May aht ee) Having to do with the multiple laws of Maat

MaatHor-NeferuRe-(May aht hor nef er oo ray/ may aht hor nef er oo rah) She who sees heru and the beauty of Ra

MaatneferuRe- (May aht nef fer oo ray/ may aht nef er oo rah) She who sees the beauty of Ra

MekentAten- (Mek ent ah ten) Behold of Aten/ protected

MerenIset-(Mer en ee set) Beloved of Auset

MerenMut- (Mer en moot) Beloved of Mut

Meresankh- (Mer es an kh) She loves life

MeresAnkhemHotep- (Mer es an kh em ho tep) She loves life and peace

Meretseger-(Mer et sejer) She loves silence

Merit- (Mer eet) Beloved one

MeritAmen-(Mer eet Ah men/ Mer eet I-men/ Mer eet Ah moon) Beloved of Amen

MeritAten-(Mer eet ah ten) Beloved of Aten

MeritHeru- (Mer eet Hair oo) Beloved of Heru

Meritites- (Mer eet et es) Beloved of her father

MeritNeith-(Mer eet Nee th) Beloved of Neith

MeritNeter- (Mer eet Net er) Beloved of god

MeritPtah- (Mer eet Pah tah) Beloved of Ptah

MeritRe- (Mer eet rah/ mer eet ray) Beloved of Ra

MeritSekhmet-(Mer eet seckh met) Beloved of Sekhmet

Mutemheb- (Moot em heb) Mut on jubaliee

Muteminet-(Moot em en et) Mut in the valley

Mutemwiya- (Moot em we yah) Mut in the divine bark

Mutnedjmet- (Moot nej met) Mut is lovely

Mutnoferet-(Moot no fer et) Mut is beautiful

<u>N</u>

Naeemah-(Nah ee mah) Benevolent one

Nefu- (Neh foo) Freedom- to breath

Nebet-(Neh bet) Lady

Nebetah-(Neh be tah) Lady of the palace

Nebetnofret-(Ne bet no fret) Beatiful lady

Nebetta-(Ne bet tah) Lady of the land

Nebettaneb-(Ne bet tah neb) Lady of all the lands

Nebettawy-(Ne bet tah we) Lady of the two lands

Nedjmet- (Nej met) Lovely

NeferAmen-(Ne fer Ah men/ Ne fer I-men/ Ne fer Ah moon) Amen is good or beautiful

NeferHenut-(Ne fer he noot) The beautiful mistress

NeferNeferAten-(Ne fer Ne fer Ah ten) Beauty of the beauties of Aten

NeferNeferRe- (Ne fer Ne fer Rah/ Ne fer Ne fer ray) Beauty of the beauties of Ra

Nefertah-(Ne fer tah) Beauty of the land or Earth

Nefertiti- (Ne fer tee tee)The beautiful woman has come

Nefertkau-(Ne fert kah oo) Beauty of souls

NefertNesut-(Ne fert nes oot) Beautiful one of the king

Neferu- (Ne fer oo) Beautiful

NeferAten-(Ne fer ah ten) Beauty of Aten

NeferuRe- (Ne fer oo rah/ ne fer oo ray) Beauty of Ra

NeferuPtah- (Ne fer oo pah tah) Beauty of Ptah

NeferuShery-(Ne fer oo sh airy) Little beauty

Neith-(Neeth) A name of a Neteret

Neithemhat-(Neeth em hah-t) Neith in the palace

NeithHotep-(Neeth ho tep) Neith is pleased

Neithqret- (Neeth ker et) Neith is excellent

Neithnofret-(Neeth no fret) Neith is beautiful

Nekhbet- (Neck bet) Woman from nekheb

NesMut- (Nes moot) She who belongs to Mut

NesNeith- (Nes neeth) She who belongs to Neith

NesNut- (Nes noot) She who belongs to Nut

NesTefnut-(Nes tef noot) She who belongs to Tefnut

NiankhBastet-(Nee an kh bas tet) She who lives for Bastet

NimaatHapi- (Nee may aht ha pee) She who belongs to the truth of Hapi

Nofret- (No fret) Beautiful woman

Nofretiabet- (No fret ee ahbet) The beautiful eastern woman

Nubnofret- (Noob no fret) Gold and beauty

Nenpetnofret- (Nen pet no fret) Young and beautiful

R

RkhtyHotep- (Rech tee ho tep) Knowledge of peace/ wisdom of peace

S

SatDjehuti-(Sah t je hoo tee) Daughter of Djehuti

SatHora- (Sah t hor ah) Daughter of Heru

SatAah-(Sah t ee ayh) Daughter of the moon

SatMontu- (Sah t mon to) Daughter of Montu

SenetMut- (Se net moot) Sister of Mut

SenetNedjmet-(Se net nej met) Lovely sister

SetepenMut- (Set ep en moot) Chosen one of Mut

SeteprenRe-(Set ep en rah/ set ep en ray) Chosen one of Ra

Shepen-(Shep en) A gift

ShepenHotep- (Shep en ho tep) A gift of peace

ShepenMut-(Shep en moot) A gift from Mut

ShepenSopdet-(Shep en sop det) A gift from the star Sirius

ShepenUpet-(Shep en oo pet) A gift from Upet

Shepset- (Shep-set) Holy one

Sherit- (Shur-eet) Little one

SitAmen- (Seat Ah men/ Seat Ah moon/ Seat I-men) Daughter of Amun

SitHut-Heru- (Seat Hut hair-oo) Daughter of Hut-Heru

SitHut-Heru-Merit-(Seat hut hair-oo Mare-eet) Daughter of Hut-Heru the beloved

SitHut-Heru-yanet- (Seat Hut hair-oo yah net) Daughter of Hut-

Heru of Innu

SitRe- (Seat-rah/ Seat- ray) Daughter of Ra

SobekNeferu- (So-bek Nef-er-oo)Beauty of Sobek

T

Taemniut- (Tah em nee-oot) She who is in the city

Taemwadsi- (Tah em wad see) She who is in her flourishing

Tasheritenlah- (Tah sher it en ee ay h) Little one of the moon

TenRe- (Ten Ra/ Ten Ray) She who belongs to Ra

TentAmun- (Tent Ah-moon/ Tent I-mun) She who belongs to Amun

TentOpet- (Tent oh pet) She who belongs to the Opet festival

U

Uaa- (Oo ah) To meditate

Uraeus- (You ray us) Name of a serpent goddess associated with the eye of Ra and kundalini

W

Weret- (Wer et) Great one

Wiya- (Wee yah) Divine bark

Y

Yabet- (Yah bet) Eastern woman

Yaret- (Yah ret) Cobra goddess

Divine Masculine Names

A

Aha-(Ah ha) Warrior

Ahmose- (Ah mos/ ah mos ay) Child of the moon

Akhenaten- (Ahk en ah ten) He who is useful to Aten

Akhenre- (Ahk en rah/ ahk en ray) He who is useful to Ra

Amaru- (Ah mah roo) Unconditional love

Amenemhat- (Ah men em hat/ Ah moon em hat/ I-men em hat) Amun is in the palace

Amenemheb-(Ah men em heb/ ah moon em heb/ i-men em heb) Amun in jubilee

Ameneminet-(Ah moon em i-net/Ah men em i-net/ i-men em i-net) Amun in the valley

Amenemopet- (Ah moon em oh pet/ ah men en oh pet/ i-men em oh pet) Amun in the opet festival

Amenemweya- (Ah men em we yah/ ah moon em we yah/ i-men we yah) Amun in the divine bark

Amenhotep- (Ah men ho tep/ ah moon ho tep/ i-men ho tep) Amun is pleased

Amenmose- (Ah men mos/ Ah moon mos/ i-men mos) Child of

Amun

Amennakht- Amun is powerful

Amenti- He belongs to Amun

B

Bak-(Bahk) Servent

BakenAmen- (Bah ken ah men/ bah ken ah moon/ bak en i-men) Servent of Amun

Bakennebut- (Bak en neb oot) Servent of his lord

BakenPtah- (Bak en pah tah) Servent of Ptah

BakenRe- (Bak en rah/ bak en ray) Servent of Ra

BakenReNef- (Bak en rah nef/ bak en ray nef) Servent of his father Ra

D

DjedefHor- (Jed ef hor) Heru is his strength

DjedefRe- (Jed ef rah/ jed ef ray) Ra is his strength

Djedi- (Jed ee) Strength

Djoser- (Jo ser) Holy

H

Hapimen- (Hap ee men) Hapi is eternal

Hapusenep- (Hap oo sen ep) Health of Hapi

HesiRe- (Hes ee rah/ hes ee ray) Favored by Ra

HorAha- (Hor ah ha) Heru the warrior

Horemakhet- (Hor em ahk et) Heru of the two horizons

Horemheb- (Hor em heb) Heru on jubilee

Horherkhopsef- (Hor her kh op sef) Heru protects him

HorHotep- (Hor ho tep) Heru is pleased/ at peace

HorNkht- (Hor Ne khet) Heru is powerful

I

ImHotep- (Em ho tep) In peace

ItAmen- (Eat ah men/ Eat ah moon/ Eat i-men) Amun is the father

Itnedjem- (Eat nej em) Good father

K

KaNefer- (Kah ne fer) Good of soul

KaPtah- (Kah pah tah) Soul of Ptah

KaWab- (Kah wah-b) Pure of soul

KhaemWaset- (Kha em wah set) Born in Waset/ Thebes

KhnumHotep-(Kh noom ho tep) Khnum is pleased

KhonsuemWaset-(Khon su em wa set) Khonsu in Waset

M

MeketRe- (Mek et rah/ mek et ray) Behold Ra/ protected by Ra

Men- (Men) Eternal

MerenPtah- (Mer en pah tah) Beloved of Ptah

MeriAmen- (Mer ee ah men/ mer ee ah moon/ mer ee i-men) Beloved of Amun

MeriAten- (Mer ee ah ten) Beloved of Aten

MeriAtum- (Mer ee ah tomb) Beloved of Atum

MeriMose-(Mer ee mos/ mer ee mos ay) Beloved child

MeriRe- (Mer ee rah/ mer ee ray) Beloved of Ra

MinMose- (Men mos/ men mos ay) Child of Min

Minnakht- (Men nah ket) Min is strong

MinNefer- (Men ne fer) Min is good

Montuemhat- (Mon too em hat) Montu in the palace

MontuemWaset- (Mon too em wah set) Montu in Waset

MontuHotep- (Mon too ho tep) Montu is pleased

N

Naeem- (Na ee m) Benevolent one

Nakht- (Na ket) Powerful

NakhtMin- (Na ket men) Powerful is Min

NakhtPaAten-(Na ket pah ah ten) Powerful is the Aten

NebAmen- (Neb Ah men/ Neb ah moon/ Neb i-men) Amun is the lord

Nefer- (Ne fer)Good/ beauty

NeferefRe- (Ne fer ef rah/ ne fer ef ray) His beauty is Ra

NeferHotep- (Ne fer ho tep) Peace is good

NeferMaat-(Ne fer may aht) Truth is good

Nehesy- (Ne heh see) Nubian

NesiAmen- (Nes ee ah men/ nes ee ah moon/ nes ee i-men) He belongs to Amen

NesiAten- (Nes ee ah ten) He belongs to Aten

NesiKhons- (Nes ee k ohns) He belongs to Khonsu

NesPtah- (Nes pah tah) He belongs to Ptah

Netjerikhet- (Net jer ik et) Divine body

NiankhPepy-(Nee an kh pep ee) His life belongs to Pepi

NiankhPtah- (Nee an kh pah tah) His life belongs to Ptah

NiuserRe- (Nee oo ser rah/ nee oo ser ray) His power belongs to Ra

NubNefer- (Noob ne fer) Good gold/ beautiful gold

P

PaekAmen- (Pah ek ah men/ Pah ek ah moon/ pah ek i-men) The servent of Amun

Paneb-(Pah neb) The lord

PaRemeses- (Pah rah mes es/ pah ray mes es) Son of Ra

Pashedu-(Pah shed oo) Shining

PenAmen-(Pen ah men/ pen ah moon/ pen i-men) He who belongs to Amun

PenNut-(Pen noot) He who belongs to Nut

PenTawer- (Pen tah wer) He who belongs to Toweret

Piankhi- (Pee ahn kee) The living one

Pinedjem-(Pen ej em) The lovely one

PtahHotep-(Pah tah ho tep) Ptah is pleased

PtahMose- (Pah tah mos/ pah tah mos ay) Child of Ptah

PtahShepes-(Pah tah shep es) Ptah is Majestic

R

RaDjedef- (Rah jed ef/ Ray jed ef) Ra is his strength

RaHotep-(Rah ho tep/ Ray ho tep) Ra is pleased

Rameses-(Rah mes es/ Ray mes es) Child of Ra

Ramose- (Rah mos/ Rah mos ay/ Ray mos/ Ray mos ay) Child of Ra

RaNefer- (Rah ne fer/ ray ne fer) Ra is beautiful or good

RaUser- (Rah oo ser/ ray oo ser) Ra is strong

RaWer- (Rah wer/ Ray wer) Ra is great

Rkht- (Rech t) Knowledge

RkhtemHotep-(Rech tem ho tep) Knowledge of peace

S

SaMontu- (Sah Mon too) Son of Montu

Sekhem- (Seh chem) Strong/ Energy

Sekhemkhef- (Sek hem kef) Strong of body

SeneMut-(Sen ee moot) Brother of Mut

SenNefer- (Sen ne fer) Lovely brother

SetepenAmun- (Set ee pen Ah moon/ set ee pen ah men/ set ee pen i-men) Choosen of Amun

SetepenRe- (Set ee pen rah/ set ee pen ray) Choosen of Ra

Seti- (set ee) He belongs to Setekh

SetekhemWeya- (Se tech em we yah) Setekh of the divine bark

Setekhi- (See tech ee) He belongs to Setekh

SetekkhNakkht-(See tech nak khet) Setekh is powerful

Shepseskaf-(Shep ses ka f) Holy of soul

ShepseskaRe- (Shep ses kah rah/ shep ses kah ray) Holy is the soul of Ra

SiAmun-(See Ah moon/ See ah men) Son of Amun

SiAtun- (See ah toon) Son of Atun

SiMut- (See moot) Son of Mut

SiPtah- (See pah tah) Son of Ptah

SaNeferu-(Sah ne fer oo) Son of all that is good/ beautiful

SobekHotep- (So beck ho tep) Sobek is pleased

T

TutankhAmen- (Toot an kh ah men/ toot an kh ah moon/toot an kh i-men) The living image of Amun

TutankhAten- (Toot an kh ah ten) The living image of Aten

TutAnkhHotep- (Toot an kh ho tep) The living image of peace

U

UserAmen- (Oo ser Ah men/ oo ser i-men/ oo ser ah moon) Amun is strong

UserKaf-(Oo ser kah f) Strong of Soul

UserMontu-(Oo ser mon too) Montu is strong

Suggested Reading

-Seeded Ascension by: Uraeus Ophaughnie Neteru Amaru Anuwi

-Egyptian Proverbs compiled by :Muata Abhaya Ashby

-Bhakti Yoga: The yoga of love and devotion by Swami Vivekananda

-Devotional Worship book of Shetaut Neter by: Muata Ashby

(and)

All other Kemetic books soon to come by Ayeri Nyah Assom

Bibliography

-Isis: Queen of Egyptian magic by: Jonathan Dee

-Ancient Egyptian Divination and Magic by: Eleanor L. Harris

-An Egyptian Hierogylphic Dictionary volume 1&2 by: E.A Wallis Budge

-Egyptian Magic by: E. A. Wallis Budge

-Sesh Medew Netcher: A beginner's introduction to medew netcher by : Wudjau Men-ib Iry-Maat

Made in the USA
Columbia, SC
27 April 2023